Journey with Jesus
A Forty Day Devotional

Copyright © 2018 by Michael Patrick Walter
Designed and edited by Dramatic Rabbit ©
Interior photos Copyright © 2018 Erin Calkins
All rights reserved.

Quotations from The Holy Bible, English Standard Version® (ESV®)
Copyright © 2001 by Crossway
All rights reserved.

This book or any portion thereof
may not be reproduced or used in any manner whatsoever
without the express written permission of the publisher
except for the use of brief quotations in a book review.
Printed in the United States of America
First Printing, 2018
ISBN 978-0-9995091-4-2
M-4 Publishing Las Vegas, NV

WELCOME

Thank you so much for choosing to participate in the next 40 days with Jesus. This devotional is intended to be supplemental to your already existent Bible study or reading plan. I pray that as you walk through these you will take the time to hear from God and apply them to your life.

HOW TO USE THIS DEVOTIONAL:

1. Read the Bible passage and make note of the focus scriptures
2. Read the devotional
3. Do the action item, which is generally a question.
4. Once you are done with these portions, I encourage you to spend some time in prayer.

I would like to thank Joy Lies for writing a handful of the devotionals as well as assisting me in this project. I also want to thank Erin Calkins for editing and formatting. Lastly, I would like to thank my wife for her patience and consistent listening to me. I love and thank you all for your support and assistance.

SCRIPTURE FOCUS

He was in the world and the world was made through Him, yet the world did not know Him. He came to His own, and His own people did not receive Him. But to all who did receive Him, who believed in His name, He gave the right to become children of God. Who were born not of the will of the flesh, nor of the will of man, but of God. And the Word became flesh and dwelt among us, and in Him we have seen His glory, glory as of the only Son from the Father, full of grace and truth.
John 1:10-14

DAY 1

Reading: John 1:1-18

He came into the world He created, it did not recognize Him, and the people He came for did not receive Him.

Think about that for a minute: The world Jesus came for and created, didn't even notice he came, and did not receive him. As a matter of fact, we reject him! He came to earth, leaving his seat in the throne room of Heaven for a world that wants nothing to do with him. However, He also knew that there would be some who would receive Him—who would become children of God.

As you prepare to set aside 40 days to draw closer to Jesus, start with the understanding that He has always existed, stepped out of His divinity, and lived among us, that we might see His glory and His great love for us.

ACTION ITEM:

What does it mean that grace and truth came through Jesus?

DAY 2

Reading: Luke 1:26-38

SCRIPTURE FOCUS:

"...For nothing will be impossible with God." And Mary said, "Behold, I am the servant of the Lord; let it be done to me according to your word." And the angel departed from her.
Luke 1:37-38

Nothing is impossible with God! This is usually the part we grab hold of, but I want us to draw our attention to Mary's response. "I am the servant of the Lord; let it be done to me according to your word." She heard something we would all call impossible, and her question is logical. She stated, "How can this be? I have not known a man." But ultimately concluded, "May it be done to me as the Lord wills."

How many times have we stopped at our 'logic'? Thinking "This doesn't make sense." Or "how will this work out?" But Mary shows us this truth we can pray. "Even though it doesn't make sense, let it be done as you say Lord, I am your servant." Take this truth today knowing that nothing is impossible for God and His Word, when we submit ourselves to it.

ACTION ITEM:
In what area has logic or reason held you back from something God has spoken?

DAY 3

Reading: Matthew 2:1-15

SCRIPTURE FOCUS:

And going into the house, they saw the child with Mary his mother, and they fell down and worshiped him. Then, opening their treasures, they offered him gifts, gold and frankincense and myrrh.
Matthew 2:11

Jesus is born and laid in a watering trough made of rock, visited by angels, and a star shines overhead. A star so brilliant some wise men see it from far away. They start a journey to find this King that they had read about. The journey takes quite some time, roughly two years. As they draw near, this miraculous star shines again and leads them to a small child. There he is, the 18-month-old King, living down and out in Bethlehem! So as all wise men do, they bow before this infant and offer gifts fit for kings and worship Him.

There is something about this story that has always made me close my eyes and try to imagine this. Adult wise men bowing to an 18-month-old in worship. The humility blows my mind, the willingness to journey for almost two years! Then they deliver the gifts—I find Gods providence here astounding. He sends some wise men on a two-year journey to provide the gifts and resource for Jesus' family to make the journey to Egypt in order to save His life.

ACTION ITEM:
Have you ever doubted Gods providence or provision? How does this story encourage you to worship?

DAY 4

Reading: Luke 2:41-52

SCRIPTURE FOCUS
After three days they found him in the temple, sitting among the teachers, listening to them and asking them questions. And all who heard him were amazed at his understanding and his answers. Luke 2:46-47

Jesus, the Son of God, sat at the feet of men to learn and ask questions— What a crazy thought! I have heard many say Jesus knew the whole Bible because He wrote it and He was the Son of God. However, as we read the Scriptures it says that He emptied himself of His Divine abilities (Philippians 2:6). I believe He sat and learned like we did. Jesus sat there asking questions and interacting with Rabbi's, teachers, simply to learn.

How passionate are you to learn and grow? Jesus understood that He was in His Father's house. Maybe He thought it was His time to start walking in what He was put on earth for. But it wasn't, and He submitted to that, to His mother and father, to the writings and teachings of humanity. Jesus was submitted and driven to grow and mature.

ACTION ITEM:

What are you doing to mature in the things of God? Are you willing to sit, learn, and ask questions?

DAY 5

Reading: Matthew 3:13-17

SCRIPTURE FOCUS
And when Jesus was baptized, immediately he went up from the water, and behold, the heavens were opened to him, and he saw the Spirit of God descending like a dove and coming to rest on him; and behold, a voice from heaven said, "This is my beloved Son, with whom I am well pleased."
Matthew 3:16-17

Imagine you're standing at the edge of the Jordan River. John the Baptist is calling people to repent, and he looks like a crazy person. You are there to watch the show and maybe even get in the water yourself. Then, this guy shows up and throws John's game off and this random guy tells John to baptize him.

What? Who is this guy? Then the guy tells John that he HAS to do this to fulfill His call. So John does it, and as the guy comes back up from the water, Heaven RIPS open and a voice from the clouds shouts, "This is my beloved Son, in whom I am well pleased." If that wasn't enough, a dove descended on the guy— It was crazy!

Could you imagine being there, hearing the affirmation of who this man was? What a sight! Imagine it from Jesus' perspective—hearing your Father in Heaven affirm you before you have done anything. Not a miracle, a sign, or a teaching. The Father just says that you are my Son and I'm pleased with you, then gives you the Holy Spirit and empowers you for ministry and with authority. What a way to start your ministry!

ACTION ITEM:

If the Father affirmed Jesus before He had 'accomplished' anything, how do you think the Father sees you? Is your affirmation in what you do for God, or is it found in the fact that you're His child?

DAY 6

Reading: Luke 4:1-14

SCRIPTURE FOCUS
And Jesus, full of the Holy Spirit, returned from the Jordan and was led by the Spirit in the wilderness. Luke 4:1

Jesus: You were just baptized, called into ministry, filled with the Spirit, and your Dad told you that He is pleased with you. Talk about a good day, right? What's the first thing that you are going to do now that you're full of the Spirit?

Go to the wilderness? The Spirit speaks! Luke says, the Spirit DROVE Him to the wilderness to fast for 40 days and be tested. Talk about an unwanted change in the day. Jesus was sent into the desert to be tested by the Spirit of God.

Sometimes in our life, the Spirit is the one leading us to be tested in a desolate place. We usually blame the devil, his demons, the world, or bad choices. But, if you are seeking after God the Father, and are listening to His Spirit, you will be sent to a deserted place and tested. If Jesus was, why wouldn't we be tested? This is an important time in our walk, embrace it.

ACTION ITEM:

Have you ever felt led to the wilderness? What did you use as your defense? How well do you hold on to God's Word as your defense and foundation?

DAY 7

Reading: Luke 4:14-30

SCRIPTURE FOCUS
And Jesus returned in the power of the Spirit to Galilee, and a report about him went out through all the surrounding country. Luke 4:14

Jesus returned in the power of the Holy Spirit.

I love this verse, it's one of my favorites! Jesus stood the test in the wilderness, and the result was the power of the Holy Spirit. I think some people who pray for the power of God have never stood the test in the desert.
God's Spirit sends us to be tested, but we often quit, or ask to be delivered from the very test that would launch us into what we have been praying for. Don't quit, stand firm, this test results in power!

ACTION ITEM:

Do you want to operate in the power of God? Have you withstood the test in the desert?

DAY 8

Reading: John 2:23-3:21

SCRIPTURE FOCUS
For God did not send his Son into the world to condemn the world, but in order that the world might be saved through him. John 3:17

We may all know John 3:16, but I love verse 17. Jesus did not come into the world to condemn sinners; He wants them to be saved. The funny thing is, if you've been a Christian for awhile you may be avoiding the world. We may interact with it on occasion, or if we have to, but we don't desire for it to be saved. Matter of fact, we are shocked that the world would act like the world. We expect the world to live according to our "morality" and get frustrated with them when they don't see things from our world view.

We are here to love the people of this world, to get involved in their life, in the midst of the messiness that comes with it and lay our lives down for them. Jesus didn't come to condemn them, so why should we? I challenge you today to ask God to see the world through the lens in which Jesus sees it.

ACTION ITEM:

How do you see the world? Do you see sinners in need of a savior or do you see people who "just don't get it"?

DAY 9

Reading: John 4:4-30

SCRIPTURE FOCUS
The Samaritan woman said to him, "How is it that you, a Jew, ask for a drink from me, a woman of Samaria? (For Jews have no dealings with Samaritans) John 4:9

The liberal, the homosexual, the homeless person—the list goes on. For almost every person, there is someone in some walk of life that we would rather not speak to. To the Jew, it was the Samaritan. Jews hated them, let alone a woman who was getting water in the middle of the day. You see this in her amazement that Jesus was even speaking to her, let alone addressing her spiritual state and telling her of the life that He offered.

Shocked. That was her response to Jesus talking to her, and that's the response many people give me when I just start talking to them. Why is it that the people of this world find the followers of Jesus the least likely to speak to them without some sort of "truth confrontation"? Jesus spoke to the unspeakable with love, even when no one else would.

ACTION ITEM:

Who is it that you don't want to talk to, and why? What are you willing to do to make any necessary changes?

DAY 10

Reading: John 4:31-38

SCRIPTURE FOCUS
Jesus said to them, "My food is to do the will of him who sent me and to accomplish his work." John 4:34

I like survival shows, especially Alone. It is a TV show where 10 people are dropped off in some deserted area to see how long they can last, the final person to tap out wins. The two biggest things that each contestant faces in the journey is mental toughness and starvation. In the last season, three people had to be pulled out for severe starvation; the winner had lost 60 pounds! It's amazing how much our body needs food to sustain itself. If it doesn't get food, it will eventually begin eating itself for energy.

The same is true for us spiritually. Many Christians eat such small spiritual portions each week they are starving. They are tired, hungry, and their spiritual bodies are eating themselves. Jesus taps into this spiritual food that which sustains Him. He said it even sustains His natural man, and then links this "food" to doing the will of the Father.

ACTION ITEM:

What sustains you spiritually? Are you well fed, or starving?

DAY 11

Reading: Matthew 4:13-17

SCRIPTURE FOCUS
From that time Jesus began to preach, saying, "Repent, for the kingdom of heaven is at hand." Matthew 4:17

Have you ever looked at your side mirrors in your car and noticed it says, 'objects in mirror are closer than they appear'? It's really easy to forget that at times, especially when trying to fit into tight spaces. I think it's that way with the Kingdom. Sometimes, we forget that it is closer than we think. Most of us go on with our daily life without thought of God's Kingdom and its proximity to us. But, that was the message Jesus proclaimed, "The Kingdom of God is near, it's close, it's at hand, it is upon you."

Gods Kingdom is at hand, and now dwells within you. You have been given access to Gods Kingdom, His protection, His provision, and His Kingship. I encourage you to go throughout your day with the mindset that the Kingdom in present and near.

ACTION ITEM:

How do you normally perceive God's Kingdom? Is it near or far from you?

DAY 12

Reading: Mark 1:16-20

SCRIPTURE FOCUS
And immediately they left their nets and followed him.
Mark 1:18

Another day fishing, another day in dad's boat. Then you hear that the new Rabbi everyone is talking about is coming— He just called Peter to follow Him. How crazy is that?! Wait, now He is calling us! Do you hear that John? We're invited too! Let's go pack up our stuff, get our money from dad, and go say our goodbyes. This is going to be epic!

Wait, you want me to leave my stuff? Don't say goodbye, or post a status update on Facebook? Just get out of the boat and follow you? What about...

Many of us have never really thought about leaving things behind. For some, they haven't left anything behind. They're trying to follow Jesus and they just put some stuff in storage or they're dragging it behind them because they don't know how to give it up. Others left behind their foul language, their drugs, and alcohol, you know, all the things I didn't want anymore. But, what about the things you do want or find security in?

ACTION ITEM:

What are you willing to leave behind? Is there anything that came to mind that you didn't want to let go of? Why?

DAY 13

Reading: Mark 1:21-28

SCRIPTURE FOCUS

And immediately there was in their synagogue a man with an unclean spirit. And he cried out... Mark 1:23

"It's okay because no one knows. It's not a big deal because everyone does it. I can still serve God and be a good Christian, this doesn't change that..." Those words have echoed in my mind more than once at different points of my walk and at the time, I genuinely believed them. I attended church, I loved God, I was a leader but truth be told, I was lying to myself and still holding onto some of my sins. The scary part was that I was okay with it. At least I was until the power of Jesus cast out those lies from my life.

It's crazy to me to think that we can appear to be 'solid Christians' and yet still hold onto sins so tightly. We watch something that isn't good, we listen to stuff that we shouldn't, we say stuff that doesn't honor God, etc. and we make excuses for why it's okay. At least we do until it's called out by the authority of Jesus. When it's exposed and cast out, that's when we are truly free to live out the call to be His disciples.

ACTION ITEM:

What are you okay with that you shouldn't be? What needs to be cast out from your life?

DAY 14

Reading: Mark 1:35-39

SCRIPTURE FOCUS
And rising very early in the morning, while it was still dark, he departed and went out to a desolate place, and there he prayed. Mark 1:35

We may often pray for the miraculous, to see God cast out the demons, and heal the blind eyes. We focus on the amazing and public areas of Gods work. However, if you look at the life pattern of Jesus He was constantly getting away to pray. I can't tell you how many times in the Gospels that it is noted that Jesus was up early, went to a secluded or mountainous place alone, and prayed.

I believe one of the greatest hindrances of seeing Gods power in public is that we have little time with Him in private. And what time we do have is sparse and timed. I am guilty of this too, as it is a product of our busy lives. We think everything is a priority, which makes nothing a priority. I think we will see Gods power when we spend time in God's presence. Dedicated, alone, secluded, and intentional.

ACTION ITEM:

What does your prayer time look like? Would you consider getting away and alone to pray?

DAY 15

Reading: Luke 5:1-11

SCRIPTURE FOCUS
But when Simon Peter saw it, he fell down at Jesus' knees, saying, "Depart from me, for I am a sinful man, O Lord." For he and all who were with him were astonished at the catch of fish that they had taken." Luke 5:8-9

I love to hike, and even more so, I love spectacular views. When I reach the top of a mountain or cliff and look out at what God has created, I marvel at Him, I'm in awe of Him.

Awe is something that is in all of us, we all awe at something. Maybe it's the latest technology, sports car, clothing brand, or TV show. We all stand in awe of God too. Many of us marvel when He does something great, but we hate being in the place where we need Him to do great things. When He shows His greatness, we should respond as Peter did; with worship, and a recognition of our sinfulness. We need Him.

Peter was in awe of Jesus in that moment; he fished all night and caught nothing. Then, a Rabbi, a Bible teacher, tells the experienced fisherman where to cast his nets. That's a bit insulting, but Peters response results in a miraculous moment. "As you say..." he throws down the net and BAM! So much fish, two boats can't contain the catch! Peter is in awe, so he worship

ACTION ITEM:

What are you in awe of? When God moves has it become common, or does it still stir you to worship?

SCRIPTURE FOCUS

Moved with pity, he stretched out his hand and touched him and said to him, "I will; be clean." Mark 1:41

DAY 16

Reading: Mark 1:40-45

There is a man I know that seems to always attract those in need at gas stations. Countless times, I have seen him approached by people in need of gas and every time, without hesitation, he pulls out his debit card and fills up their tank. One day, I asked him why he does it, and he responded, "If I was ever in need, I would hope someone would show me the same compassion as I have for those who I have helped." This man is moved with compassion for others, that is why he gives when most people won't.

Jesus was moved with compassion many times throughout scripture. So much so that He even reached out and touched a person that the rest of society wouldn't even let get within a stone's throw of them. Jesus looked past the world's view of the man as an undesirable and saw his value and worth. He saw him as a person made in the image of God. Jesus knew that the real value of a person is inside, not outside, and that truthfully, we are all lepers due to sin. His willingness to look past the outward appearance and social norms changed this man's life, countless other lives, and mine.

ACTION ITEM:

How about you? How often are you moved with compassion for others? Do you see undesirable people and help them, or do you do your best to keep them away?

DAY 17

Reading: Luke 5:27-32

SCRIPTURE FOCUS

And leaving everything, he rose and followed him. And Levi made him a great feast in his house, and there was a large company of tax collectors and others reclining at table with them... "I have not come to all the righteous but sinners to repentance." Luke 5:28-29, 32

Tax collectors— the scum of the first century. Can you believe them!? Taking Jewish tax dollars for the un-holy Romans. They were in their own category, tax collectors and sinners. Talk about low. Then the new Rabbi in town has the audacity to call one of them to follow him. The outrage! Then this Jesus has dinner at his house with all his sinner friends. How can this man be a righteous rabbi? He eats with sinners and tax collectors, and even invites them to follow him.

Jesus was a friend of sinners. Are you? Now, I am not saying you should go out and live immorally in order to make friends "for the sake of evangelism." What I am saying is have you had your neighbor over for dinner? What about the friends of your kids? Do you live among the people of this world and only know how to give an invite to a church service or church event? That's not the way of Jesus. He lived and served all the people around Him without living like them. He brought light and scolded the self-righteousness of the Pharisees.

ACTION ITEM:

Are there any "sinners" in your sphere that you can love? What holds you back?

DAY 18

Reading: Matthew 5:1-12

SCRIPTURE FOCUS
Blessed are you when others revile you and persecute you and utter all kinds of evil against you falsely on my account. Rejoice and be glad, for your reward is great in heaven, for so they persecuted the prophets who were before you. Matthew 5:11-12

Live blessed! I am blessed! These are common responses from one Christian to another. But, what does this mean exactly? According to verse 11, "I am blessed when others would call me cursed." It says that I am to rejoice and be glad when people utter false things against me, hate me, and accuse me. That's not the blessing I am used to thinking about.

Maybe we should redefine how we think about blessings. Look at the passage of scripture again: Blessed are the poor in spirit, those who mourn, the meek, the persecuted, and more. Now hear me out, I am not saying that financial and other blessings are bad, but we need to recognize everything that God calls blessed. You are blessed when you are opposed for the Gospel, when people don't like you because of who you serve. Remember, when these things happen, you are blessed for being meek not combative, it is the Lord who avenges.

ACTION ITEM
Do you live with this mindset of being blessed? Write down one way that you are blessed with this passage of scripture in mind.

DAY 19

Reading: Matthew 5:13-18

SCRIPTURE FOCUS
You are the light of the world. A city on a hill cannot be hidden. Nor do people light a lamp and put it under a basket, but on a stand, and it gives light to all in the house. In the same way, let your light shine before others, so that they may see your good works and give glory to your Father who is in heaven. Matthew 5:14-16

When I visited my sister in Colorado several years ago, we went and visited an old mining cave. This cave went about 150 feet down into the earth. The guides shared stories of how the miners would go in with a single lantern and explore these caves. Talk about crazy! At one point, they told everyone to put their phones and flashlights away and preceded to turn off all the lights. Talk about dark! I couldn't see my hand in front of me. It was scary dark. Take your breath away dark. Then one guy took out his phone, and it lit up several feet of space. That phone in his pocket made no difference, but out in the open it made a huge difference.

You see, sometimes as Christians we focus on how bright of a light we can be. We want to be a bright light for Jesus, but we don't focus on where the light is placed. Placement is as important as brightness. Jesus notes that you don't place the light under a basket, but on top of a stand.

ACTION ITEM:
Is there a basket over your light? Do your good works shine before the outside world?

DAY 20

Reading: Matthew 5:21-37

SCRIPTURE FOCUS

But I say to you that everyone who is angry with his brother will be liable to judgement; whoever insults his brother will be liable to the council; and whoever says, 'You fool!' will be liable to the hell of fire...But I say to you that everyone who looks at a woman with lustful intent has already committed adultery with her in his heart. Matthew 5:22,28

I have never personally murdered anyone or committed adultery outwardly. Here Jesus was standing in front of a crowd of people who could say the same things. 'I am righteous or good because I have never done these sorts of things...' But, Jesus challenged them and us. He's saying, 'if you have done it in your heart, if you have hated, called someone an idiot, looked at a person lustfully, you are guilty of the outward.' You see, Jesus didn't come to give us better morals, to be nice to people outwardly, but to reveal how desperate we are inwardly.

ACTION ITEM:

Take this time to repent today and ask the Spirit to cleanse and forgive you. We need His grace daily. Ask the Holy Spirit to search your heart. Ask the Lord to reveal any inward impurities.

DAY 21

Reading: Matthew 5:38-48

There you are, minding your own business and a soldier grabs you and says, "Carry this!" How dare they! It's not your shield. Why should you have to carry it! The law says you have to legally carry it a mile… but that's all! These guys treat you bad and then they want you to do something to help them! Just wait… one day they'll get what's coming to them! Then it hits you. Jesus said, "Carry it two miles." Obviously, Jesus must not realize how badly these guys treat you… why would He say that?!

He said it because after one mile, it is a choice. A choice to show kindness to your enemy. A choice to give them a gift they don't deserve, just as you were. A choice to show compassion as Jesus did. It's hard to choose love when you don't feel love. But, that's when we truly reflect Jesus. When we lay down our rights and what is deserved and choose to repay good for evil.

ACTION ITEM:

What do you do when someone wrongs you? Do you repay them with blessings or do you repay them with what you think they deserve?

SCRIPTURE FOCUS

"But I say to you, Love your enemies and pray for those who persecute you." Matthew 5:44

DAY 22

Reading: Luke 10:25-37

SCRIPTURE FOCUS
He said, "The one who showed him mercy." And Jesus said to him, "You go, and do likewise." Luke 10:37

There were two things that Jesus did (or didn't) do that upset the Pharisees the most often. Healing on the Sabbath, and not upholding to their ceremonial cleanliness. You see, in order to understand this parable, you have to understand the gibe Jesus is giving them.

We usually hear this text harp on the busyness of the priest and the Levite, but the truth is, that's not why they didn't stop. They didn't stop because the law forbid it. A priest and a Levite were not supposed to touch open wounds, as it would make them unclean. They would have to go through the entire process of becoming clean again. To them, the process of becoming clean out-weighed helping the bloody man, and the law was of more importance than kindness. So Jesus posed the question, which one did the right thing? The one who showed mercy. Go and do likewise.

ACTION ITEM:

Which of the three are you? Would you clean this man's wounds and pay his bills?

DAY 23

Reading: Luke 11:1-13

SCRIPTURE FOCUS
What father among you, if his son asks for a fish, will instead of a fish give him a serpent; or if he asks for an egg, will give him a scorpion? If you then, who are evil, know how to give good gifts to your children, how much more will the heavenly Father give the Holy Spirit to those who ask him!" Luke 11:11-13

"Dad! Dad. Hey Dad…" "Ugh! What do you want?" If you have kids, you know exactly what I am talking about. The persistent, constant, need of attention and communication. They can wear us down like running water on dry soil. And, as much as I hate to admit it, I get annoyed all too easily.

In looking at this parable, Jesus talks about the persistent and constant 'harassment' in prayer. He basically says to bother Him: Ask. Seek. Knock. Can you imagine, the Father wants to hear us say, "Dad! Dad. Dad…" And, not only that, we get a glimpse into His nature, he calls Himself a good Father who desires to give us the Holy Spirit. What a great gift!

ACTION ITEM:

Do you view God as an annoyed father or a father who anticipates you talking to Him? Do you see God as a good Father who wants you to have His spirit?

DAY 24

Reading: Luke 12:22-31

SCRIPTURE FOCUS
And which of you by being anxious can add a single hour to his span of life?...Instead seek the kingdom, and these things will be added to you. Luke 12:25,31

Is there going to be enough to get through until our next paycheck? How am I going to pay for that? I look over at the clock. It's late, but my mind won't shut off. Is what I did good enough? Are they going to get us more help to complete the tasks they are requesting of us? I check the clock again. Sigh—I can't sleep. How can I make this work? What am I going to do? Another night with little sleep means another morning of exhaustion. I can't keep this up. All this worrying is wearing me down. I get on my knees and beg God to work it all out. That's when He whispers to me, "Go to bed, I got this."

God knows our needs. He knows our struggles and He knows what is going on. Nothing takes Him by surprise so why do we keep trying to worry ourselves into solutions? His word tells us that He will take care of all our needs but wants are another story. The only thing we have to do for Him to take care of us is to seek the Kingdom of God above all else. That's it, that's the solution to all our worries. Seek His Kingdom.

ACTION ITEM:

Are you a worrier? If so, ask yourself, how much do I really trust God? If you aren't a worrier, ask yourself, am I seeking Gods Kingdom above all else?

DAY 25

Reading: Matthew 7:12-20

SCRIPTURE FOCUS
"For the gate is narrow and the way is hard that leads to life, and those who find it are few... You will recognize them by their fruits. Are grapes gathered from thornbushes, or figs from thistles?"
Matthew 7:14,16

"Is this cantaloupe good?" I ask the well-matured woman next to me. She replies with a "No." and proceeds to show me how to tell if the cantaloupe is ripe. I have never been good at knowing when fruit is ripe, maybe it is an art. I do however, know when fruit it bad. I don't think many have that issue either, but the worst is when you bite into a piece of fruit that looks good but is bad on the inside. Yuck!

You see, Jesus spoke to the people of His day plainly and in ways we can all understand. The few people who choose the narrow way, which is hard it says in verse 14, will be seen as ones bearing good fruit. Jesus never said it would be easy, but He did say it would be noticeable.

ACTION ITEM:

Take a moment to reflect on verse 14. What does this mean to you? Do you spend more time looking at your own fruit, or the fruit of those around you?

DAY 26

Reading: Matthew 5:38-48

SCRIPTURE FOCUS

"I can do nothing on my own, As I hear, I judge, and my judgement is just, because I seek not my own will, but the will of him who sent me." John 5:30

'Only God can judge me.' How many times have you heard that said, or even seen it tattooed on someone? I used to think that way too, I think we all have at some point. The truth is, that is a scary thought. Jesus says He judges by what He hears the Father say. Jesus even says He can do nothing by himself, that He only seeks the will of the Father who sent Him.

God never tells us to never make a judgement about things or people. He just warns us that to the measure that we judge we will be judged. But, if we adopted the words of Jesus here, that He only seeks the will of the Father, and to judge according to the Fathers will, maybe our judgements would look different.

ACTION ITEM:

When you make judgements, is it with your will in mind or the Fathers? Ask the Spirit to show you His perspective on making judgements.

DAY 27

Reading: John 6:22-40

SCRIPTURE FOCUS

Jesus said to them, "I am the bread of life; whoever comes to me shall not hunger, and whoever believes in me shall never thirst. But I said to you that you have seen me and yet do not believe." John 6:35-36

'I am'. Generally, what follows this phrase gives a unique descriptive that expresses an identity for that person. Jesus gives us several "I am" statements in the book of John, which give us a glimpse into the characteristics of His nature. He calls himself the bread of life, and says He is better than the manna received in the days of Moses. His bread is eternal.

One thing that I love about scripture is that there is so much depth. Here, Jesus says He is the bread of life and that He will quench any thirst. Something most people don't realize is there were a few reasons Jesus was born in Bethlehem. Bethlehem means 'House of Bread' like a bakery. So, the bread of life was born in a bakery and laid in a feeding trough. So, not only does He fulfill these things in the natural at His birth, He fulfills them Spiritually in us.

ACTION ITEM:

Do you seek Jesus as if you're starving or thirsty? If Jesus is the bread of eternal life, who is around you that can use that bread?

SCRIPTURE FOCUS
Again Jesus spoke to them, saying, "I am the light of the world. Whoever follows me will not walk in darkness, but will have the light of life." John 8:12

DAY 28

Reading: John 8:12-29

Have you ever turned off the lights to your room and felt like it was pitch black? You stumble across the room and put your hands out as to make sure that you don't run into anything on your way to bed. Then, after you have laid there for a minute, your eyes adjust, and as you open them, you can see everything around you. The room isn't any less dark, your eyes have just adjusted to it.

Sometimes, it's like that for us spiritually. It's not that we stop following Jesus, it's just our eyes have adjusted to the darkness around us. What once seemed so dark now isn't as dark as it once was. Our vision has adjusted to the darkness of this world, of this life, of our circumstance. However, Jesus calls us to see things differently, to fix our eyes on Him, the Light of the World, so that we will not be in darkness.

ACTION ITEM:

Have you let your eyes adjust to the darkness of what's around you? How can you draw closer to the light today?

DAY 29
Reading: John 10:1-21

SCRIPTURE FOCUS
So Jesus again said to them, "Truly, truly, I say to you, I am the door of the sheep... I am the good shepherd. The good shepherd lays down his life for the sheep... I am the good shepherd, I know my own and my own know me."
John 10: 7, 11, 14

It's funny how God does things so backwards from how mankind views things. In most cultures throughout history, the shepherd has been the outcast or lower- class occupation. When Israel was brought to Egypt at the request of Joseph, they requested the land of Goshen because to the Egyptians shepherds are an abomination. But as irony would have it, most of the great men in the Bible were shepherds. Abel, Abraham, Isaac, Jacob, Moses, David, and obviously Jesus himself.

You see, a shepherd's job has little glory. It's dirty, it's isolated, and it's dangerous. You have to know the sheep, where to water them, lead them to food, keep them safe, and make sure they stay together. There is no glory; there is no honor before man. You can almost hear it in David's brother's voice when he told him, "Go take care of those few sheep you have." (1 Samuel 12:28 paraphrased) Shepherding is not the occupation of choice to this world. But, our Lord calls himself the Good Shepherd and Gate Keeper. The protector of His sheep.

ACTION ITEM
:If Jesus is the shepherd, and we're the sheep, do we trust Him to lead us? Do you live in such a way that you know and hear your Shepherd's voice?

DAY 30

Reading: John 11:17-44

SCRIPTURE FOCUS
Jesus said to her, "I am the resurrection and the life. Whoever believes in me, though he die, yet shall he live, and everyone who lives and believes in me shall never die. Do you believe this?" John 11:25-26

"You are the Messiah, the Son of God who has come into the world! I believe you are the resurrection and the life…" proclaims a sorrowful Martha. She knew that if Jesus had been there, her brother wouldn't have died. As they get her sister and head to the tomb where they laid their brother four days ago, Mary also shares the sentiment, "If only you had been here Jesus…"

As they arrive at the tomb, Jesus instructs them to roll the stone away from the tomb. But Martha interrupts, "He's been in there four days! He is going to stink."
Here is what I observe… Martha, who just heard Jesus say He is the resurrection and the life and proclaimed herself, "I believe!" "You're the Messiah." has already doubted her statement. And, Jesus in His patience reminds her, "Didn't I tell you, that if you believe that you'll see the glory of God?"

ACTION ITEM:
What has Jesus told you that you say you believe, but when the time comes, you doubt? Do you ever take the time to reflect that you have eternal life?

DAY 31

Reading: John 14:1-14

SCRIPTURE FOCUS

Jesus said to him, "I am the way, and the truth, and the life. No one comes to the Father except through me. If you had known me, you would have known my Father also. From now on you do know him and have seen him." John 14:6-7

'How do we get there Jesus? We don't know the way.' I think we have all felt that, both in the natural and spiritual. I mean, most of us couldn't get anywhere without GPS these days. So, when Thomas wants to know the directions do you blame him? And, Phillip just wants to see the Father, who wouldn't, right?

Jesus' responds, "I am the way, the truth, and the life. No one comes to the Father except through me. (Oh, and by the way), if you've seen me, you've seen the Father." Jesus is both the directions and the revelation. He reveals His nature as the way to the Father, the truth regarding the Father, and life with the Father. Jesus is both the reflection of the Father and the avenue in which we get to Him.

ACTION ITEM:

Take a minute to thank Jesus. Thank Him for revealing what the Father looks like and for giving us access to Him. What does it mean to "know" God?

DAY 32

Reading: John 15:1-8

SCRIPTURE FOCUS

"I am the true vine, and my Father is the vinedresser... I am the vine; you are the branches. Whoever abides in my and I in him, he it is that bears much fruit, for apart from me you can do nothing." John 15:1,5

Life and nutrients are found in the vine, it is the lifeline to the rest of the vine. No branch can produce fruit apart from the vine. The branches and the fruit are not in charge of the rest of the plant. As long as they stay connected, they will bear fruit as a byproduct. The branch is unable to 'work harder' to make the fruit a certain way, bigger, or faster. The branch is the conduit from the vine to the fruit. You are the branch.

Fruit happens. I think we can get so fixated on bearing and producing fruit that we forget that fruit is a byproduct of being connected to the vine. You see the abiding is the most important part. Jesus tells us to abide 6 times in this passage. Abiding in Him will produce all that we need to bear fruit. Like I said, it will just happen as you remain in Him.

ACTION ITEM:

What does it mean to abide in Jesus? Do you get more focused on producing fruit than you do remaining in Him?

DAY 33

Reading: Luke 19:28-44

SCRIPTURE FOCUS

And when he drew near and saw the city, he wept over it, saying, "Would that you, even you, had known on this say the things that make for peace! But now they are hidden from your eyes. Luke 19:41-42

Rejoicing, celebration, and triumph! The people from the surrounding areas who had come for Passover were overjoyed that their Messiah had come. However, only the city celebrates; Jesus weeps over Jerusalem. Could you imagine, riding into the city as it celebrates you and honors you, but you know what's about to happen?

Sometimes, I wonder what Jesus felt. He was fully human and fully God and knew that their joy was about to be turned to hatred, and a calling for His death. The disciples, who have followed for so long, would soon depart from Him. Jesus was weeping while the city was rejoicing. Jesus was broken with the betrayal that was at hand. He knew what going into Jerusalem meant in that moment, what it meant for his earthly body and emotions, but He also knew what it meant for humanity.

ACTION ITEM:

Take a moment to reflect on what it meant in that moment for Jesus to ride into the city that would call for his death days later. Have you ever thought of Jesus' ability to empathize with how you feel when you are hurting?

DAY 34

Reading: Luke 8:4-15

SCRIPTURE FOCUS
"As for that in the good soil, they are those who, hearing the word, hold it fast in an honest and good heart, and bear fruit with patience."
Luke 8:15

In our minds, we are all the good soil. Who really wants to think of themselves as being the rocky or thorny ground? The thing about these two types of ground is that the seed actually takes root for a while. One has no root, so the seed sprouted but never took, and as Jesus said; "They believe for a while and in time of testing fall away." The other seed took root and began to grow, but as it grew the cares of this world, riches, and the pleasures of this world choked it out. Every Gospel uses the word choked to express what Jesus was saying. It literally means that the seed was strangled by the things of this world and was unable to mature.

The final soil was able to bear fruit. It was able to endure and hold fast with patience. The final soil was different regarding its ability to not give up and not allow itself to be choked out. I don't know about you, but I don't know how many times I have felt like the soil who gets choked out. The cares of this life and finding too much pleasure or 'satisfaction' in the things of this world have an appeal to our flesh. And, it's not an overnight thing, it's gradual, over time. Then, before you know it, you can't breathe.

ACTION ITEM:

Are there things in this world that could choke out the seed God has planted in you? Pray that God would remove the thorns or rocky soil that could be in your life.

DAY 35
Reading: Mark 9:33-50

SCRIPTURE FOCUS
And he sat down and called the twelve. And he said to them, "If anyone would be first, he must be last of all and servant of all." Mark 9:35

Growing up, I wanted to be like Jerry Rice or Barry Sanders. Then, I wanted to be the lead singer of a band. And then, I wanted to be a famous BMX rider or a famous snowboarder. You see, I like most kids, wanted to be seen as great. Whatever field we are in, many people want to be the greatest. We want the seats of honor. We want everyone to know who we are. Greatness is in our DNA because our Father is great.

We see this with James and John, two young disciples who at one point have their mom ask for a position in the kingdom for them. We see all of them discussing who was going to be greatest as they walked to Capernaum. So, Jesus calls them out on their conversation.

The thing that I see in Jesus' response is that He doesn't correct their desire to be great. He never once says, 'Don't desire that', instead He tells them how to be great. I think, what He tells them is actually harder than telling them to knock it off. He tells them to become the servant of all, to be last. How weird to us that greatness is found on the ground, in a position of humility. Serving people is the key to be the greatest in the kingdom.

ACTION ITEM:
What does serving 'all' look like to you? Does this mean everybody? Not just in our church buildings? Pray, Lord help us serve as you served.

DAY 36

Reading: Matthew 22:1-14

SCRIPTURE FOCUS
But when the king came in to look at the guests, he saw there was a man who had no wedding garment. And he said to him, "Friend, how did you get in here without a wedding garment? And he was speechless. Matthew 22:11-12

The day has finally come! The invitations have been sent and everything is ready. All you have to do is wait for the guests to arrive then its celebration time. Then comes the news that no one's coming. OUCH! That hurts. You recover and invite the 'B' list guests, but they too decline. Now you're upset. You've worked so hard to prepare and no one has chosen to come. At this point, you're ready to take anyone willing to come, all they have to do is show up, dress up (with the clothes you provide them of course) and eat up. Finally, people arrive, but then there's someone who chooses not to wear the wedding clothes you've provided. That just won't do. They either change or leave. There is no other option.

God has prepared a wonderful celebration for us and all we have to do is 'show up, dress up, and eat up.' It's our choice though whether we are willing to change for the banquet. We can choose to dress ourselves in the righteousness needed to enter God's Kingdom or choose not to. Either way, it's up to us. The choice is ours.

ACTION ITEM:
Have you chosen to clothe yourself in righteousness? If not, what is holding you back?

DAY 37
Reading: Luke 14:25-35

SCRIPTURE FOCUS
"If anyone comes to me and does not hate his own father and mother and wife and children and brothers and sisters, yes, and even his own life, he cannot be my disciple. Luke 14:26

'You cannot be my disciple.' These are the words of Jesus when great crowds accompanied Him. Jesus lays it out... if you don't love Him more than all that you hold dear (i.e. family, your own life) and renounce all that you have, you are not fit to follow Him. That's a hefty call, the call to give up everything for His sake. Many have never done this, they think they're following Jesus, but He reveals that we cannot half-heartedly follow Him.

There is a cost to follow Jesus. Jesus tells us to count the cost, because the cost is great. Let me clarify this though, our salvation is a free gift by grace through faith. What that means is Jesus paid the price for our sins, and conquered death, giving us access that we otherwise did not have. So, the price has been paid, but when we come to Jesus He offers His life in exchange for ours. That's the cost, our life for His, our will for His, our sin for His righteousness. That's the beauty of it— we receive the life and righteousness of the only perfect one who can stand before the Father without fault, fully justified. Our cost is us—our sin, shame, punishment, our mind, will and emotions. We lay our life at His feet, thus the saying, my life is not my own.

ACTION ITEM:
Have you counted the cost to follow Jesus? What if it cost you everything? Have you surrendered completely?

DAY 38

Reading: Matthew 26:26-29 & Mark 14:32-42

Let me take a moment and encourage you to make some time to take communion with your family. Many of us take it with our church family at a service, but there is something powerful in gathering your spouse and kids around and observing our common- union. When we take the cup, let us think of the cup Jesus referred to in the garden of Gethsemane.

Jesus labored in prayer in the garden and asked the Father if it was possible to remove the cup from Him. Now, I don't think Jesus feared the cross, the beatings, and the torture. He knew this was coming, but there was something that had him praying.

The cup Jesus referred to was the cup of wrath. This cup is spoken of several times in the Old Testament, but we see it in its full context in Revelation 14:10. Here an angel proclaims the wrath of Gods anger against those who did not believe. This cup was the cup of God's wrath against sin, our sin. For the first time in Jesus' life, He would feel the weight of sin, thus temporarily being separate from the Father. That had never happened before in Jesus' life. God poured out His wrath, His judgement, and His righteous anger on Jesus when He went to the cross. So, when you take the cup of communion, remember the cup of wrath that Jesus took for you.

Take a few moments to meditate on what this means and thank God for His great mercy and Jesus for His sacrifice.

SCRIPTURE FOCUS
And he said, "Abba, Father, all things are possible for you. Remove this cup from me. Yet not what I will, but what you will." Mark 14:36

ACTION ITEM
Have you chosen to clothe yourself in righteousness? If not, what is holding you back?

DAY 39

Reading: John 19:1-42

SCRIPTURE FOCUS
But one of the soldiers pierced his side with a spear, and at once there came out blood and water. John 19:34

If you have ever watched the Passion of Christ and seen the scene where Jesus is beaten and crucified, you'll relate that it is hard to watch. Understand this about me; I don't get queasy at violent movies, broken bones, and the like. But there is something about this scene that is hard for me to watch. It's not so much the violent nature of it, but I think it's the fact that I know in my soul that what Jesus is going through in that moment should have been me. That was my punishment, my humiliation, and my suffering He took upon himself.

He emptied himself of His deity and heavenly comfort when He came to earth (Philippians 2:7), but it was on the cross he emptied himself of what made him human, of what held his life, and what the payment of sin was. He emptied himself of all His blood. When the soldier stuck Him with the spear, water came out. Medically, what that means is that there was no blood left in His body. He had literally poured out all His blood for us, just like a sacrificial lamb in the Old Testament. He was drained out of all that made Him human as a sacrifice. Jesus saying, "It is finished!" showed that God was satisfied with the sacrifice, the debt of humanity's sin was paid.

ACTION ITEM:
Worship. Pray. What does Jesus being the Passover lamb mean? What ramifications does this have on your daily life?

DAY 40

Reading: John 20:1-18 & Matthew 28:16-20

SCRIPTURE FOCUS
Jesus said to them again, "Peace be with you. As the Father has sent me, even so I am sending you." John 20:21

As the Father has sent me, even so I am sending you!' Jesus' resurrection proved He was who He said He was. He was the first-born among many who would have eternal life. This is good news! So, Jesus charges His disciples as apostles, or ambassadors of this Good News. Go into all the world! He has charged all those who follow Him as carriers of the message of the Gospel to the world. We are foreigners, going into the world that we know, telling them about this message our King sends, that life is available to all.

I know sometimes it's a struggle to view ourselves with that kind of call, authority, or ability. But, that is Jesus' call and intention for each one of us, to live and proclaim the Gospel. You don't have to be a theological expert, a pastor or leader, or have any sort of earthly qualifications to declare what Jesus did on the cross. Read the Gospels, that's what we proclaim, who Jesus is and trust the Holy Spirit to do the rest. Keep the good news the good news, you can do it!

ACTION ITEM:
Do you view yourself as a courier of the Gospel? If not, why not? Don't let fear hold you back from the mission God has given you.